NOW YOU CAN READ ABOUT....

THINGS THAT GO

TEXT BY STEPHEN ATTMORE

HARRY STANTON AND MARJORIE ROGERS

ILLUSTRATED BY TONY GIBBONS

BRIMAX BOOKS • NEWMARKET • ENGLAND

INTRODUCTION

We are sure you will like this big book. It is about things that go. There are things that go on land, things that run on rails, things that float on water and things that shoot into space. You can read about Spacecraft, Trains, Cars and Trucks, Robots, Space Travel, Planes, Ships and Rescue From Danger. Look at the super pictures. You will learn a lot from this book.

Now you can read about . . . THINGS THAT GO.

© Brimax Rights Ltd 1985   All rights reserved
Published by Brimax Books, Newmarket, England.
ISBN 0 86112 279 8
Printed in Portugal by Edições ASA—Divisão Gráfica

CONTENTS

SPACECRAFT

We have lift-off! Up goes the rocket. Look for the spacecraft at the top. It is only a small part of the rocket. Huge tanks full of fuel are below it. This spacecraft is on its way to the Moon.

10   9   8   7   6   5

How does a space rocket move? It is like a firework rocket. Fuel is burned inside. This makes hot gases. Look for the stream of hot gases escaping from the rocket. The force of the gases pushes the rocket along.

This space rocket has three
stages. As each stage runs out of
fuel, it falls away. The next stage
fires. Then the space rocket can
go faster. It goes higher and
higher. Look for the spacecraft
on its own. It is now in space.

Here is Robert Goddard standing
beside the rocket he built in
America. It flew for two seconds.
It reached a height of 12 metres.
Well, that was a record in 1926!

In 1957 the
Russians sent
this strange
thing into orbit.
As it circled the
Earth, it sent out
radio signals.
One year later
the Americans
sent a satellite
into space. Here
is the rocket
before lift-off.

This Russian spacecraft is called Vostok 1. The artist has cut away part of the spacecraft. Look for the pilot. He was the first person to go into space. The round bottles were filled with air. The pilot breathed this air.

The year is 1969. This American spacecraft is in orbit round the Moon. The landing craft is going down on to the Moon. Two men are inside it. They are the first humans to visit the Moon.

This is a Russian space station.
Teams of Russians are taken up in
smaller spacecraft. They stay at
the space station for many days.
The long arms are solar panels.
They take heat from the Sun and
make it into electricity.

This American space station is Skylab. The solar panels are like the arms of a windmill. Look for the spacecraft about to link up with Skylab. The people inside the small spacecraft are going to work at the space station.

The space shuttle
is a space plane.
It takes off like
a rocket, but
lands on a runway.
This American
spacecraft can go
up into space
many times.

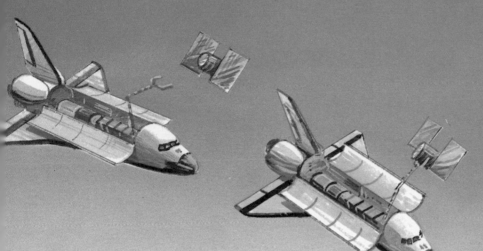

Look for the
space shuttle
picking up the
satellite. A long
arm is reaching
out. Then the
satellite is
loaded inside the
space shuttle.

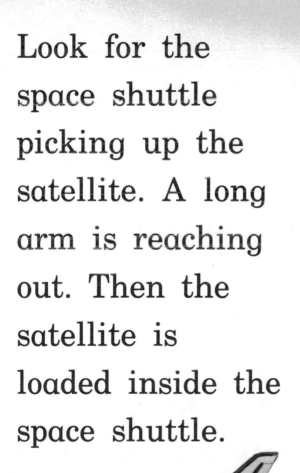

Look at this spacecraft falling
back to Earth from space. It is
re-entering the air around our
planet. The spacecraft is going
very fast. It is getting very hot.
It has a special heat shield.

The spacecraft has splashed down in the sea. Look at the outside of the spacecraft. The heat shield is damaged. It is peeling off. This happened when the craft re-entered the air around Earth.

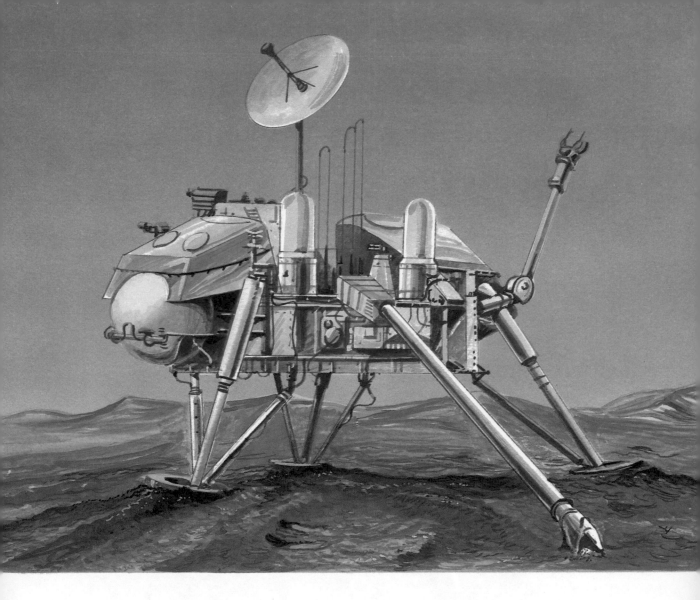

This American spacecraft is
a long way from Earth. It is on
the planet Mars. Look at the red
sands and pink sky. Some planets
are a long way away. Spacecraft
travel for years to get to them.

This Russian craft is going through the air above Venus.

This American craft is flying past the planet Mercury. It looks like the Moon.

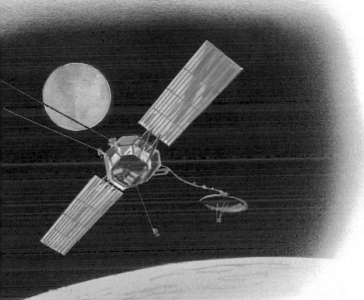

Here is Voyager 1 passing Saturn. The rings are made of millions of small rocks covered with ice.

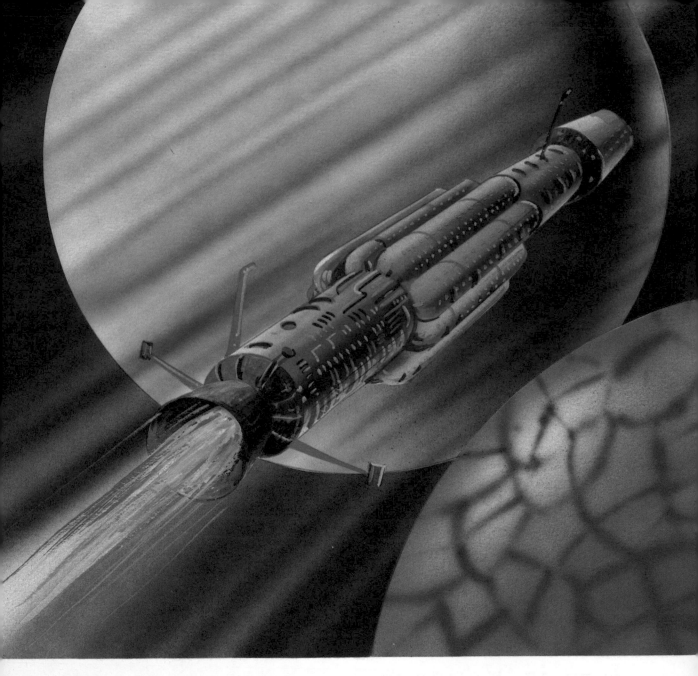

What will happen in the future?
Perhaps spacecraft will travel to
the stars. They are so far away
that we will need a very powerful
rocket. It might look like this.

One day people might live in giant spacecraft. Look at this monster craft. Would you like to live in space?

In this chapter you have read about spacecraft. Can you name these space vehicles? What are they doing?

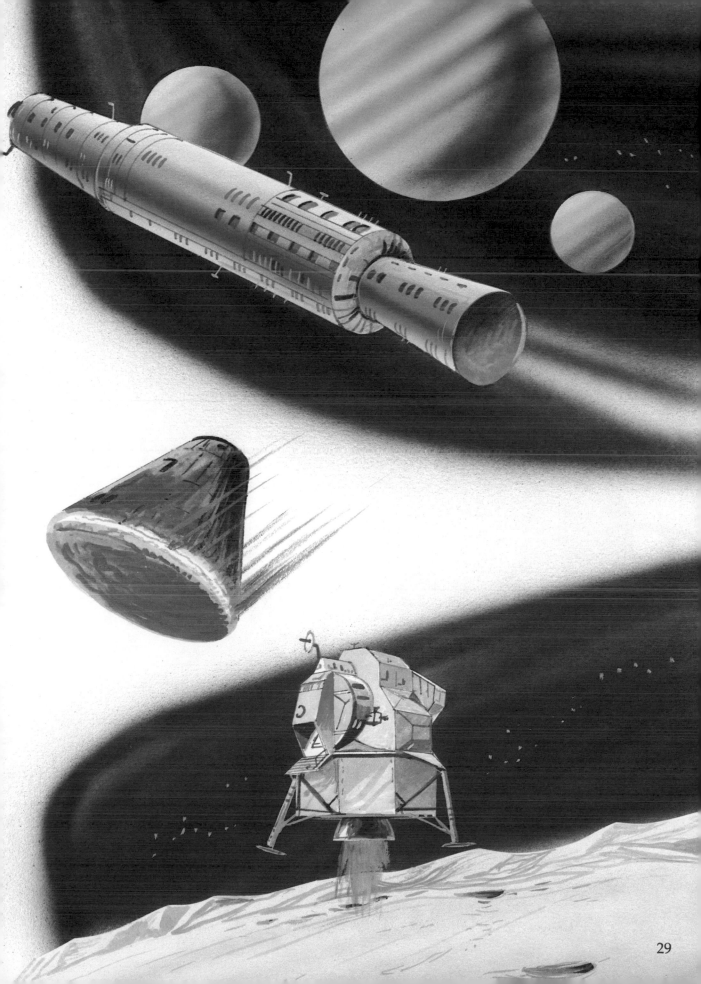

TRAINS

Here is a busy railway station.
Can you see the people waiting?
When the train comes in to the
station the people get inside.
Then the doors are closed.
The guard waves his flag.

A big express train rushes past.
There are many people inside.
The signals change from red to
green. Now the train can leave
the station. The engine starts
to pull the train. The engine
makes a loud noise.

This is the driver of the train.
He is in his cab. Look at all
the dials and levers.
The driver has his hand on a
handle. When he moves the handle
one way, the train goes faster.
When he moves it the other way,
the train slows down.

When the driver wants to stop
the train, he pulls on a lever.
This lever works the brakes.
The driver has one foot on
a pedal by the floor. If he
takes his foot off this pedal,
the engine will stop working.

This man is in a signal box.
He watches lights on a long
board. These lights show where
each train is. As our train moves
along the rails, the lights
move along the board. This is to
make sure that two trains do not
meet on the same track.

The signalman flicks a switch.
The signal lights in front of
our train change.
A signalman can warn a train
driver of danger. He presses
a button in the signal box. This
makes a bell ring or a light
flash in the cab of the train.

Some trains do not run on level tracks. They can climb steep hills like the one here. One train is joined by a cable to a second train. As one train goes up the other train is pulled down the hill.

Here is another way for a train
to get up a steep hill. The metal
rail has teeth. These teeth grip
a wheel under the train. This
train runs on only one rail. It
is called a monorail.
Most trains run on two rails.

Others are used to carry goods.
They are called goods trains
or freight trains. They can
carry cattle, cars, fuel, coal
and grain.
These engines pull many box-cars
or wagons. Flat ones carry cars.

40

Some carry coal or grain. These
are called hoppers. They can
tilt over on one side. The coal
or grain then falls out.

Many years ago, trains were pulled by steam engines. They burned coal or wood in a firebox. The fire heated water. Steam from the hot water worked the engine.

The train going over the bridge ran in America. Wood was burned in its firebox. Can you see the big chimney? This stopped sparks from the fire doing damage.

Here is the first train to carry
people. It was called "Rocket".
It first pulled a train over
150 years ago.

Steam trains began to go faster
and faster. They had bigger
engines and a smooth shape to
help them go faster.
Look at the large silver train.
It looks like a long cigar. It
was made in America.

In England there were many fast steam trains. Here is the "Mallard". At one time it was the fastest engine in the world. These engines became too big. They could not carry enough coal. In the end, these engines ran out of steam.

The big engine above is a high speed express. Diesel fuel makes its engine work. It takes people across Canada. The journey lasts many days.

Look at the railway coaches or cars. Some have beds in them. People sleep in them at night.

This train is from Germany. It is an electric train. It picks up its power from the wires over the track. This means the train does not have to carry fuel. Electric trains are lighter and faster than other engines.

This is a very fast electric train. It takes people in France on their holidays. The engine in the front is very big. It has great power.

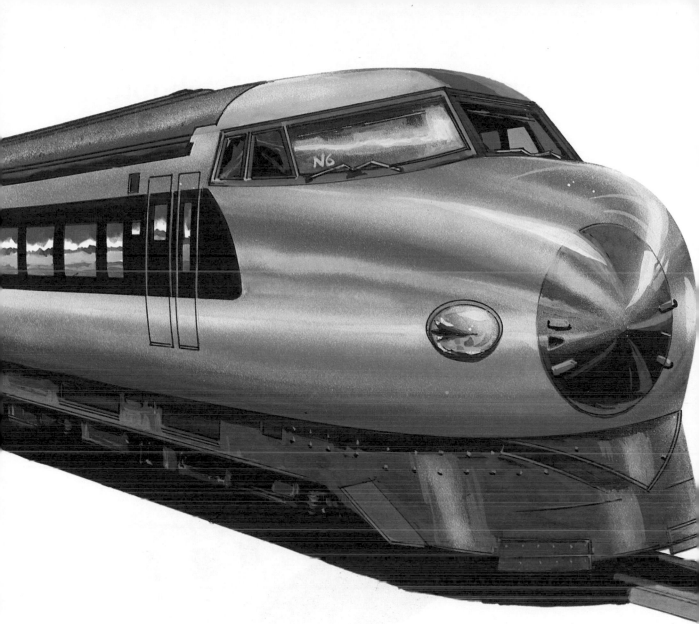

In Japan trains travel 400 miles at over 100 miles an hour. Each night workers look at the track. They make sure that the trains and the people in them will be safe next day.

All these appear in this chapter.

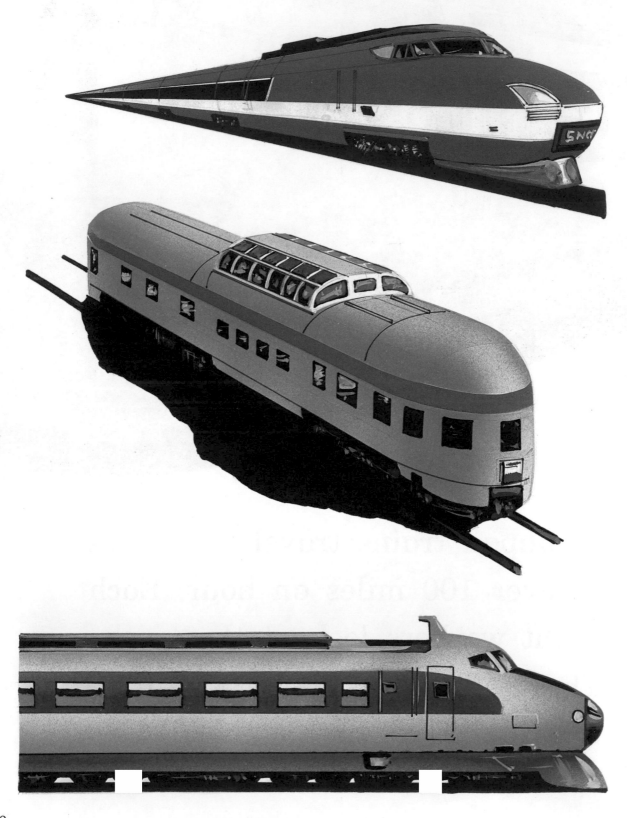

What kind of trains are they?

CARS and TRUCKS

These people are looking at the
cars and trucks. These cars and
trucks are for sale. Each year
there are more cars on the roads.
In some countries people
drive on the left side of the road.
In North America and Europe
cars and trucks go on the right.

Trucks are used to carry loads.
They move things from place to
place. Some trucks are used
to take goods from the factory to
supermarkets and stores.

Look at the two cars. The small car cannot go very fast. It is better to drive a small car on short trips. It does not use as much fuel. The large car has more room inside. It can go fast. Some people like to drive big cars when they go on long journeys.

There are trucks to carry every
sort of load. Trucks can go to
almost any part of the world.
The large truck is a juggernaut.
It can carry large loads for long
distances. The small truck carries
little loads on short trips.

Here is one of
the first cars
ever made. It is
over 80 years old.
The brakes on
this car are not
very good. If you
want to stop it
on a hill, you use
a sprag. It is
like an anchor.

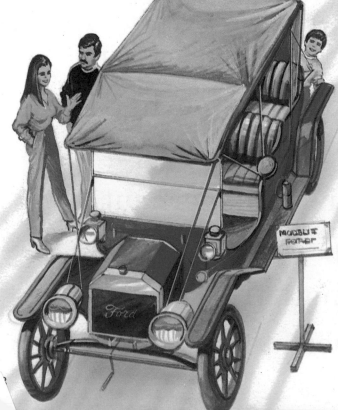

This car was made
in America. It is
a Model T Ford.
Over 15 million
of these cars
were sold.

Here is a 1906 Rolls Royce Silver Ghost. The engine was so well made that it was as quiet as a ghost.

This is a German car. It is called a Beetle. More people have owned a Beetle than any other make of car.

Have you been to a car museum?

Here is one of the first trucks
ever made. The driver and the
goods are in the open. Look for
the handle at the front of the
truck. This is turned to start
the engine. The wheels are wooden.

This American truck was made 70 years ago. It keeps the load and the driver dry. But it is cold for the driver in winter. Look for the gas lamp. This is the headlight. This truck has rubber tyres.

Look at this modern tanker. It is
carrying a large load of fuel.
Other tankers carry milk, wine or
gases. The driver is talking to
other drivers on a CB radio.
The driver can sleep in the area
at the back of the cab. Count the
number of wheels on the truck.

This is inside a modern car. Look
at all the dials. One dial shows
the speed of the car. Another dial
shows how much fuel there is left
in the car. This car also has
a computer. Its controls are to
the right of the steering wheel.
It can speak to you.

Most cars are built to travel on
roads. But some cars can travel
where there are no roads. You can
drive this Range Rover car over
rough ground. The engine has a lot
of power. This car's tyres grip
on land where other cars' tyres
would get stuck.

Many trucks are used to carry
loose loads like coal, sand and
gravel. The yellow truck is called
a dumper. Its strong engine pulls
it over rough ground. The other
truck is a tipper. It is not as
strong. Tippers and dumpers can
tip up their loads.

Lights flashing,
sirens blaring
this is a road
accident in Britain.
The police are
there first. They
will try to find
out what happened.
Fire fighters are
putting out the
fire. Fire engines
are special
trucks. Ambulances,
fire engines and
police cars can
go fast. They get
to the scene of

an accident as soon as possible. The ambulance is taking the people who are hurt to hospital. These cars and trucks must have good engines. It is no help if they will not start or if they break down. People or animals may be in danger. Can you see the breakdown truck towing a car?

This is a sports car. There is
only room inside for two seats.
It can go fast. Rally cars drive
along rough roads. The drivers try
to get from one place to another
as fast as possible.

The modern racing car is passing
the old racing car. They are on
a special track. You can see how
racing cars have changed. Here is
a strange car. It is called a drag
racer. It goes very very fast.

What do you think cars and trucks
will look like in the future?
Here are some ideas. The long car
is a special shape. This makes it
go faster and saves fuel. The tyres
are special too. They will not
burst. The small car uses
electricity for fuel.

This is what a truck of tomorrow
might look like. Look at its shape.
Its engine is quiet.

Now you have read about cars and trucks in this chapter. What are these cars and trucks used for?

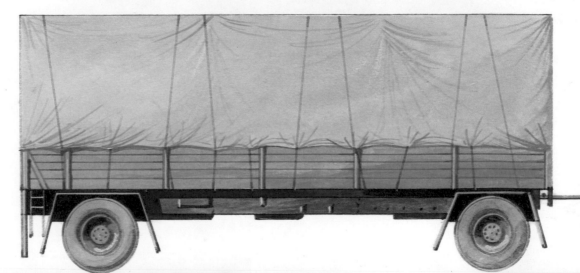

ROBOTS

What is a robot? Today we know robots as machines we can program. This program gives them a set of actions to follow. We use robots to help us work and play. They can move in many ways. They are lots of shapes and sizes.

We often think of robots as metal humans.

The word robot refers to work and workers. It was used first in a play 60 years ago. Look at this actor. He is acting the part of a robot. The robot is working in a factory.

The first robots were very simple.
They could not work by themselves.
They had to be worked by people.

Shadow puppets
were worked by
moving thin sticks.

This string puppet
moves its arms
when the strings
are pulled.

This toy was made over 200 years ago. It could play chess. At first people thought it was very clever. Then they found out that a tiny man was hidden inside.

This music box plays pretty tunes.

Pascal's adding machine was made over 240 years ago. It helped people add up sums. It made mistakes like you or I.

This metal man was driven by steam. Look at the steam pouring out of the cigar.

Many early robots had to be wound up. This clever toy could play the violin. As it played it turned its body and tapped its foot. At the same time it fluttered its eyelashes.

Sometimes on television and in films we see robot men and animals. These are like the early robots. They have people hidden inside them. They are acting like robots.

These children are playing robots. Can you move like a robot?

This car has a computer.
Its voice tells people to fasten
their safety belts. It also speaks
when a door is left open.
The computer cannot hear you if
you speak to it.

Some things we use at home could be called robots.

An automatic washing machine is a kind of robot. It has a program. You can choose how to wash clothes. Sometimes it uses very hot water, sometimes it uses cold water.

Video recorders can be set to record from a television. They switch on at the right time and the right channel. They can switch off by themselves.

This sewing machine has many programs.

Robots are used
in factories.
This robot helps
to build cars.
It has a computer
into which a
program is loaded.
Look at the robot
arm. It can turn
in many directions.
On the end of the
arm is a tool.
The tool welds
parts of the cars
together.

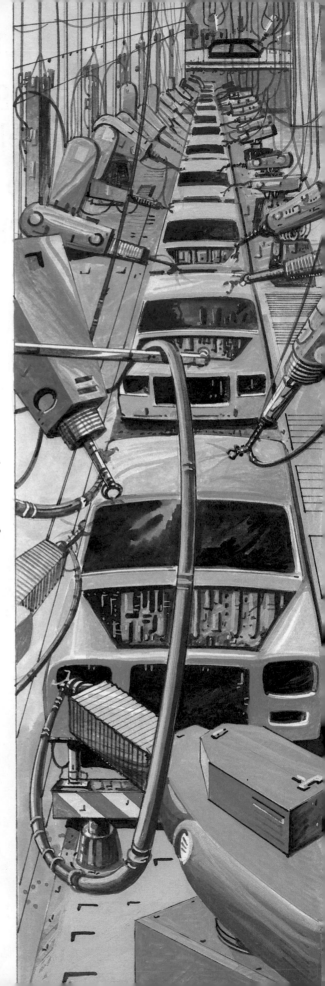

Different tools
can be fitted
to the robot's arm.

Look at the robot
spraying paint on
to the car body.

Robots work very
carefully. They
cannot get tired.
They can work for
weeks without
stopping.

Like puppets, these robots are worked by people.

This machine is called a Mobot. Can you see its metal arms and fingers? Instead of eyes it has a television camera. This shows the person in the next room what the Mobot is doing. He can control the Mobot. It is mixing chemicals which must not be touched.

This robot is used by the army.
It searches for bombs. On the
front is a television camera.
The arm at the front can open
doors. It can also break windows.
The robot can carry bombs to
a safe place.

Robots are used in places where people cannot live. Strange machines work deep under the oceans. This machine is used to repair broken oil pipes. This robot collects samples of rock from the ocean bottom. Look for the lights on the front of the underwater robot.

Some robots are sent into space.

In 1970 this robot car was sent to the Moon. It collected samples of rocks. This was before astronauts were able to go to the Moon.

What robots shall we see in the future?

Soon only a few people will be needed to work in factories.

Perhaps trains and buses will run without drivers.

We may have
machines to buy
our food, store it
and cook it.

Will we have
robot servants
who will look
after us?

Would you like
a robot to
play with?

In this chapter you have read about
these robots. Can you name them?
What do they do?

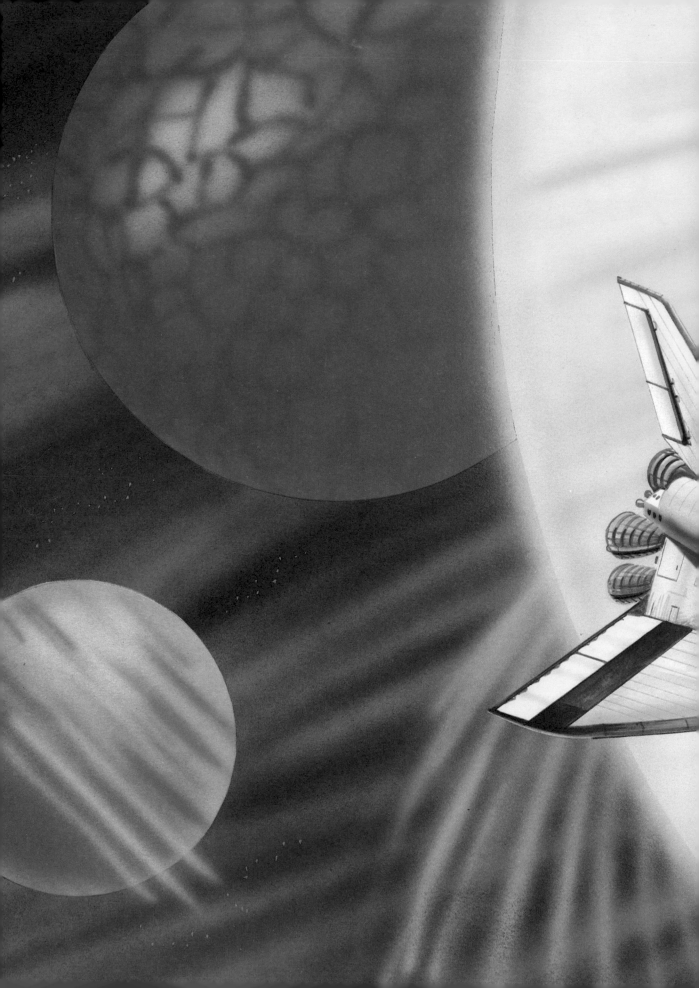

SPACE TRAVEL

10

9

8

7

6

5

4

3

2

1

We have lift-off! Here is the American space shuttle. It has three engines and two extra rockets. They all fire together. Look for the big fuel tank. The shuttle is taking people up into space.

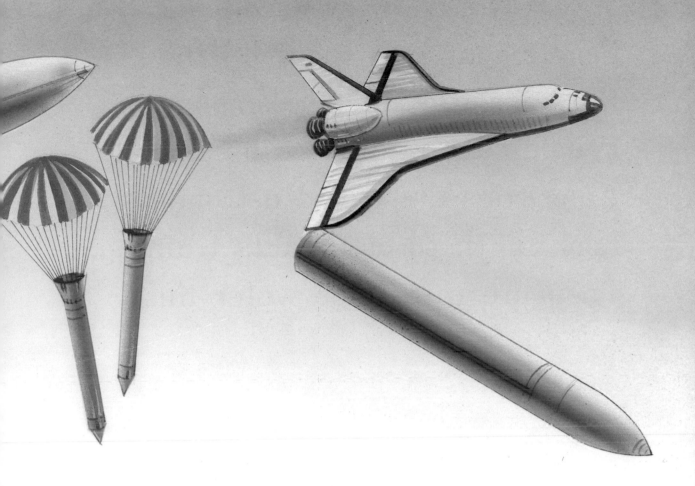

About two minutes after lift-off
the shuttle lets the booster
rockets go. They fall down to
Earth. Six minutes later the fuel
tank is dropped. It is empty now.
When it is in space the shuttle
orbits the Earth. It goes round
and round us.

People sent into space by the
Russians are called cosmonauts.
People sent into space by the
Americans are called astronauts.
Look at these astronauts training.
They are in a huge water tank.

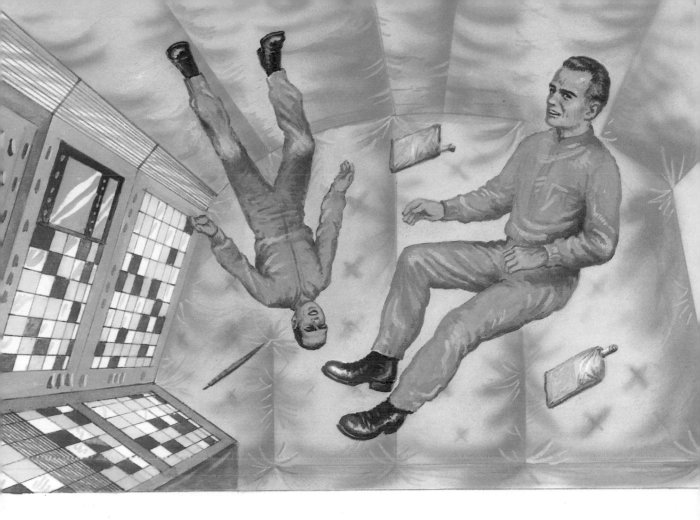

What happens when you throw a ball
in the air? It comes down again.
A force called gravity pulls it
down to Earth. People in space
find that there is no gravity.
Look at the people floating in
their spacecraft. If they let go
of something it floats away.

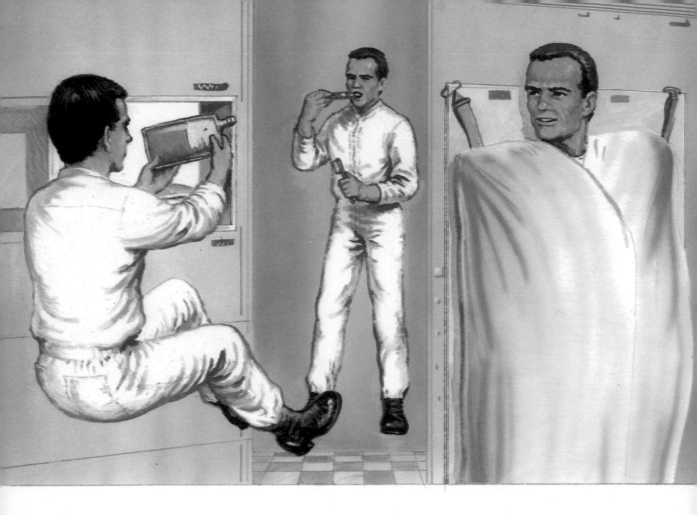

Life in space has its problems!
Food is kept in special packs.
You cannot pour drinks into
glasses. You squirt the drink into
your mouth. People in space cannot
sleep in beds – they and the bed-
clothes would float away. Look at
the astronaut in a sleeping bag.

Look at this astronaut. He is space walking. The long tube leads from the craft to his spacesuit. He breathes air through it.

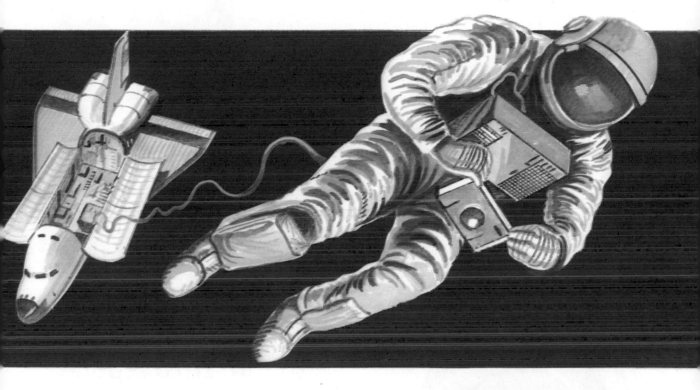

Can you see the special pack worn by this astronaut? He can move away from the craft.

A dog called Laika was the first space traveller. She was sent into orbit by the Russians in 1957. Laika stayed in space for seven days.

The first person to go into space was a Russian. In 1961 Yuri Gagarin circled the Earth in a spacecraft called Vostok 1.

John Glenn was
the first American
to go into space.
He circled the
Earth in 1962.

A year later the
Russians sent the
first woman into
space. Valentina
Tereshkova went
round the Earth
48 times.

On 20 July 1969 an American
spacecraft landed on the Moon.
Astronaut Neil Armstrong climbed
down a ladder. He was the first
person to step on to the Moon.
He was followed by Edwin Aldrin.

Look at this astronaut driving
a strange car. It is a special car
for getting about on the Moon.
Can you see Earth in the sky?

Look at the cosmonauts inside the house in space. It is a space station. The cosmonauts live and work here. They do tests to find out about space. After a few weeks they return to Earth. Then other cosmonauts go to the space station.

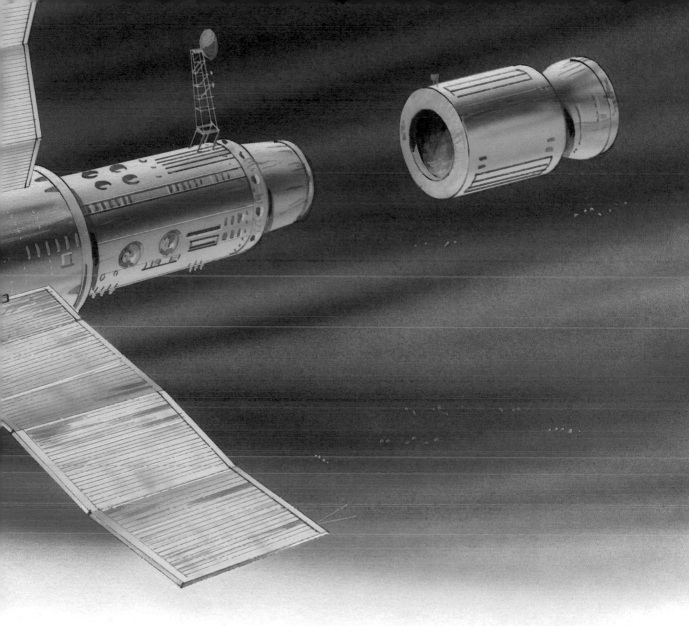

Can you see the small spacecraft
about to dock? It is going to join
up with the space station. There
are no people on board the small
craft. It is bringing food, water
and fuel. It has come from Earth.

In July 1975 astronauts met
cosmonauts in space for the first
time. American and Russian
spacecrafts joined together.

Parts of the two crafts are not shown. Look for the Americans and the Russians shaking hands. Which ones are the cosmonauts?

These astronauts have splashed
down in the sea. They are back to
Earth. The big balloons on the
American spacecraft help it to
float. A rescue boat is on its way
to pick up the astronauts.

When the space shuttle returns to Earth it lands like a plane. It uses its wings to fly. The space shuttle lands on a runway.

Russian space-craft come down on land. As they get near to Earth, the cosmonauts eject. They are thrown out of the spacecraft.

What will space stations be like in the future? This one looks like a city in space. A space shuttle is carrying people from Earth to the space station. It will take other people back on its return.

Will people live on the Moon?
Many years from now, people may
live in a Moon city like this.
Think about it. You may be able
to take a holiday on the Moon!

In this chapter you have read about people in space. What are these people doing?

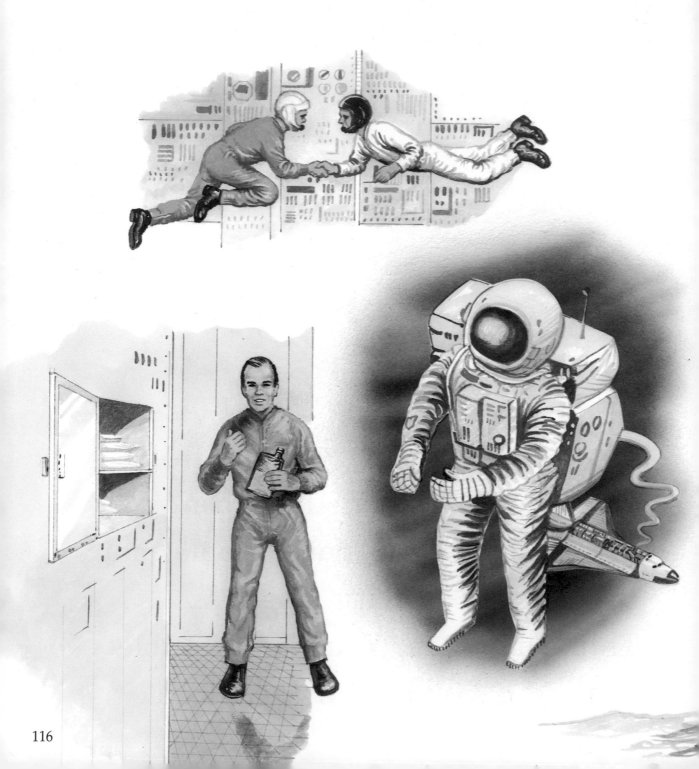

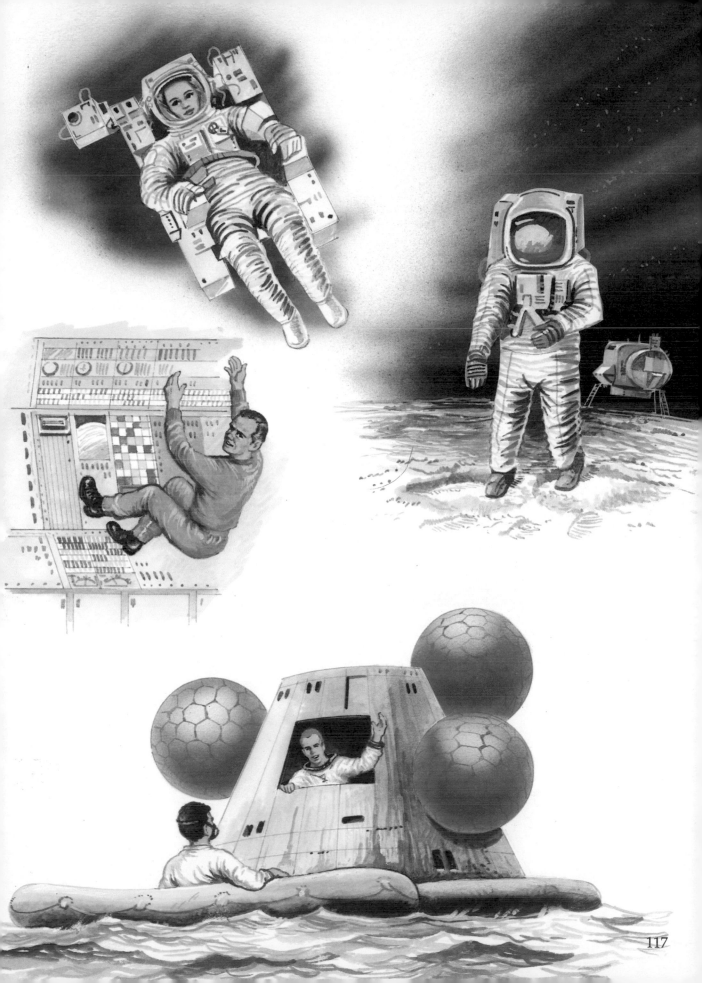

PLANES

For many years men have wanted to fly like the birds. Some tried by fitting wings to their arms and jumping off high places. Some filled balloons with hot air and floated in them. They could not stay up in the air.

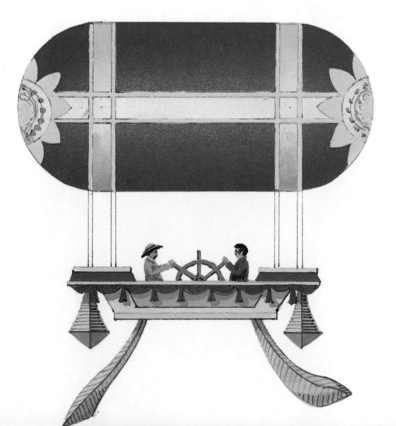

Men found that a plane must have
wings to lift it, a tail to keep
it steady and an engine to give
it power. Over seventy years ago
in America, an engine was fitted
into a glider. The first short
flight was made.
Planes can now fly all over the
world and even out into space.

This is an airport. Planes need
runways for taking-off and
landing. Can you see the planes?
Some are in parking bays or gates.
This is where people get on or off
the planes. Before taking-off, a
plane will need fuel.

Fuel for the planes is stored in
big tanks on the airport.
Airports are very busy places.
Many people work there. They take
care of the people who fly in and
out every day and night. On the
airport there are large buildings.
There people can wait for flights,
shop and have meals.

This is the pilot.
He flies the plane.
He sits at the
controls in the
cockpit. The pilot
uses levers to
control the engines
and parts of the
wings and tail.

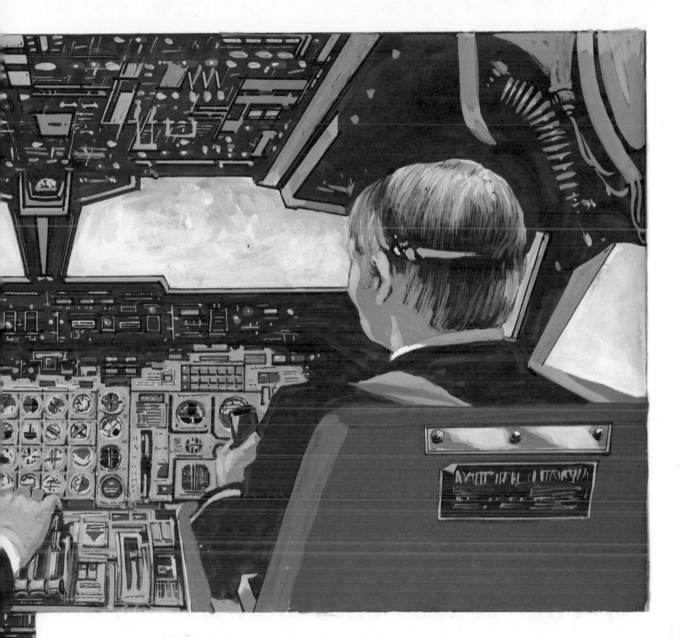

Look at all the dials. They show
the pilot what the plane is
doing as it flies. The man
who sits with the pilot to help
him is called the co-pilot.

This is the control tower. The
people who work here help the
pilot. They can speak to the
pilot of each plane over the
radio.

They make sure that all the planes take-off and land on the right runway. They tell the pilot all about the weather. There is a plane ready for take-off.

The people who travel in an airliner sit in the cabin. The cabin crew serve food and drinks during the flight.

On long flights, you can watch a film and listen to music.
Under the floor of the cabin is the hold. This is where all the bags and cargo are stored.

Concorde is a very
special plane. It has
swept back wings
and a droop nose. It
can fly very fast
and very high.

This plane has a
very wide body. It
is called a Jumbo
Jet. It has seats
for hundreds of
people. This kind
of plane is known
as an airliner.

The Jump jet does not need a runway. It takes-off and lands straight down on the ground. It is the first jet that can do this.

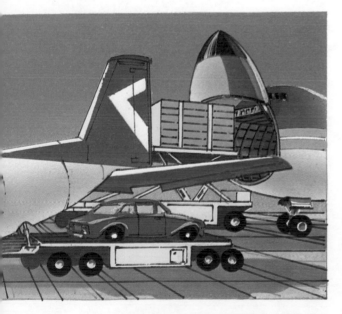

A cargo plane can open at the front or back. It can carry heavy loads.

This plane has a metal body built like a fast boat. It can land and take-off on the sea, to ferry goods and people over the water. It is a sea-plane.

A helicopter is lifted into the sky by its blades. It can hover using the blades and the engine to keep it steady. It can be used to save people in danger.

Only one person can fly in this plane. It is used to spray crops. Spraying kills pests and weeds.

This airliner is inside a large
building. It is called a hangar.
Here many men work to make the
plane ready to fly. All the parts
of the plane must be in working
order.

After a flight, repairs to the plane
can be made in the hangar. This
is to make sure that the plane
is safe to fly once more.

The first rockets to the moon were only used once. The space shuttle has been made so that men can use it again and again. It will be able to shuttle between the earth and a space station.

In the next few years, who knows at what speed planes will fly or what they will look like.
Perhaps they will look like these.

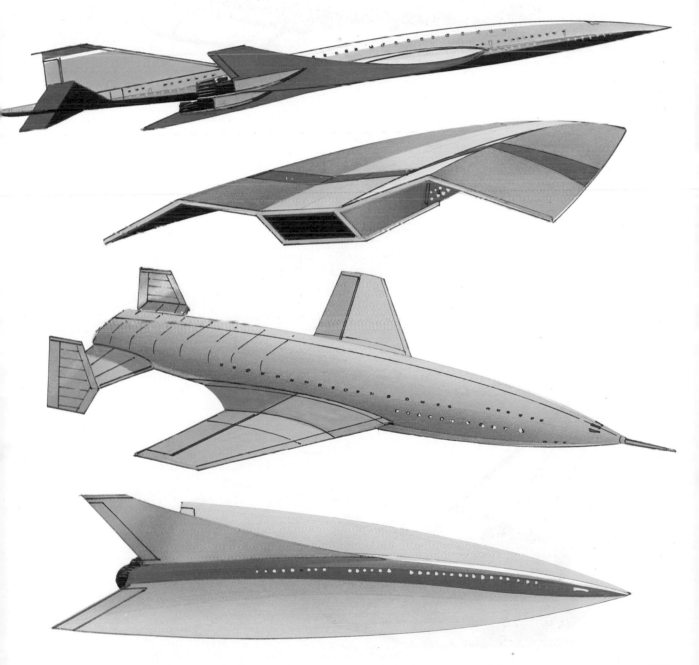

Can you name these? What kind of
planes are they?

SHIPS

Look at these ships. Have you seen
ships like these on the sea?
Long long ago, people tied logs
together to make rafts.
A paddle was used to move
and steer the raft.
The people who went out on these

boats were very brave.
Then people learned to use sails
to make their ships move.
But sails need wind. What did
they do when the wind dropped?
They rowed. The rowers were called
galley slaves. Look for their oars.

Bigger and better ships sailed
on the sea. They sailed for days
on long journeys to lands
far away. There they met people
who spoke strange words.
These ships were made of wood.
Look for the big square sails.
Bigger ships carried more people.

New ships called warships were
built. Speed was needed, whether
there was a strong wind or not.
They had rows of oars.
Later the big ships had cannons.
Great battles were fought
on the sea.

Steam engines began to be used more and more. Galley slaves were not needed then. Early steamships had sails as well. The sailors had to use the sails when the engines broke down.

Steamships had paddle wheels.
Look for the big wheel on
this ship. Most of it is out
of the water.

This big ship was called a liner.
It carried lots of people.
Now they were able to travel to
many places over the sea.

You can see all sorts of ships
today. Some are big, some
are small. This little tug
is very strong. It is pulling
a large liner into port.
The liner is a floating hotel.
It travels around the world. Over
2,000 people can stay on it.

Ships have become bigger and bigger. This huge tanker takes oil from country to country. It is too large for most docks.

It stops out at sea. Pipelines take the oil on and off.

Can you see a sail? These ships have big engines to power them.

This ship is always busy.
It is a ferry. It carries
people and their cars.

This is a lifeboat. It is used
to rescue people.
It is often called out during
storms at sea.

The ship with the big lamp
on its mast is a lightship.
It warns other ships of danger.
Lighthouses also warn ships.
They are sometimes on the land
and sometimes on rocks at sea.

This is a busy port. Ships
tie up at the dock here. Then
people get on and off. There
are many buildings at this
port. Goods are stored here
for loading on to the ships.

Look at the container ship
tied up in the dock. There are
big boxes on its deck. These
boxes can be easily loaded
and unloaded.

At the docks,
big cranes lift
heavy loads.
They lift the
big boxes on
and off the
container ships.
This crane is
putting an
engine on to
the deck of
a ship.

This is a special dock. Trains
can be driven on to the ferry.
It can only be done when
the rails on the dock and on
the ship join up.

Warships today are made of metal.
They carry huge guns. These guns
can fire large shells which can
go a long way.

Look at the planes on this ship.
It is an aircraft carrier.
There is only a short runway
for the planes.

This is the bridge of a ship.
From here the captain controls
the ship. The captain gives
orders to his crew.
Look at all the dials and levers.
Can you find the wheel?

Long ago, captains found their
way at sea by watching the sun
and stars.
Now they use a compass and radar
to find their way.

What can you see in these pictures?

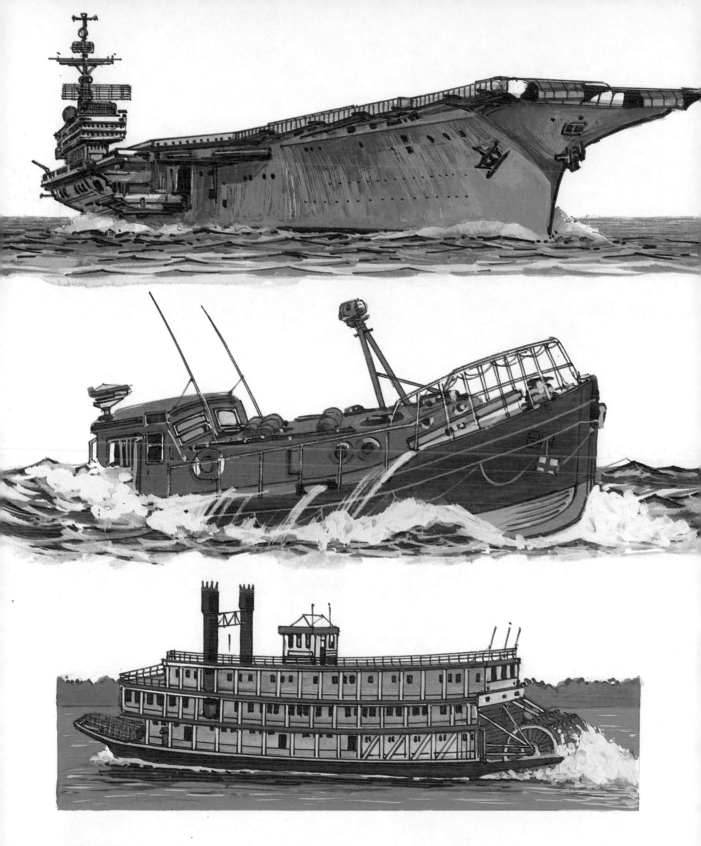

Can you name these ships?

What else do you know about them?

RESCUE FROM DANGER

There has been an accident.
Someone has been hurt.
The ambulance is rushing to
hospital. Can you see the
light flashing on the ambulance?
It is also sounding its siren.

At night the police rescue truck uses its powerful light. Afterwards the light is lowered down into the truck.

The police are helping to rescue people. They are directing the traffic and putting out signs.

This is one of the
first ambulances.
It was used 200
years ago by the
French army. Two
wounded soldiers
could be carried
in the ambulance.

Long ago rowing boats were used
to rescue shipwrecked sailors.

This is one of the first fire engines. It was pulled by fire-fighters to the fire. The hoses were made of leather. Many people were needed to work the pumps.

Look at this steam pump. It was made nearly 100 years ago. It was pulled by horses.

This fire engine can carry ten men.
It has a pump that can spray water
to the top of high buildings.
It also has a large tank of water
used to put out small fires.

Look at the people
at the top of the
building. They are
trapped. The long
ladders are used
to bring them down.

This Ladder Truck is used in
America. When it is driven the back
wheels also have to be steered.

At an airport fire trucks are always ready. They have very powerful engines. They can race along the runway to help an aircraft that has crashed.

The fire truck carries enough water to fill a small swimming pool. The water is mixed with a chemical to make foam. It is sprayed onto the aircraft to put out fire. The foam also stops a fire starting.

In Australia many farms are hundreds of miles from the nearest doctor. When a person has an accident or becomes ill, the farmer talks to a doctor by radio. The doctor tells him how to care for the patient.

If someone is very ill, the Flying
Doctor will visit him by plane.
Look at the patient on the
stretcher. The Flying Doctor
is taking him to hospital.

S.O.S. Someone needs help. The yacht is sinking. The crew race to the lifeboat. The boat is launched within minutes. The people will soon be rescued.

The ship is sinking. People are lowered into the sea in small boats. Another ship is coming to their rescue. The Captain is always the last person to leave a sinking ship.

A diver is trapped
under the sea.
This tiny submarine
will rescue him.
Only two or three
people can get
into it.

This strange ship puts out fires on oil rigs. Look for the big hoses. Smaller hoses keep the ship cool when it is close to the fire. They spray water on to the sides of the ship.

These tugs are used to put out fires on ships.

Help! Someone is injured and cannot move. A helicopter has come to the rescue. The pilot is keeping the helicopter steady. They are lowering one of the crew on to the mountain. The injured man will be lifted up into the helicopter.

What rescue machines might we see in the future?

Space shuttles are used to repair satellites. Perhaps one day a space shuttle will be used to rescue astronauts.

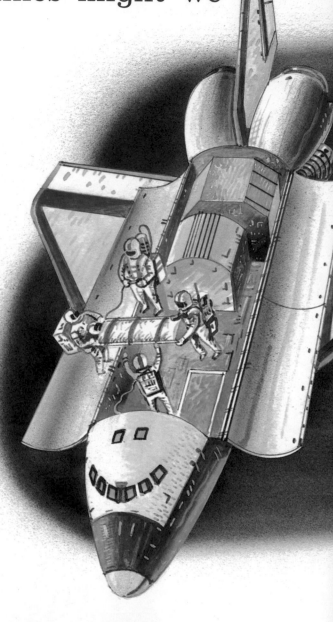

Will we see robot fire-fighters? They may be able to go very close to the fires.

Look at this machine. Perhaps it could rescue trapped miners.

One day rescue teams may wear special back packs. Then they could fly to rescue people from danger.

All these rescue machines are in
this chapter. Can you name them?

In this book you have read about trains, cars, planes, travel in space, ships, robots and rescue. Now you can find out about giant machines, the fastest and the slowest.
You can see more things that go on land, on water and in the air.

Have you ever seen a hot air balloon? Did you know that there is a strange ship that flips on end? Now you can read **more about . . .**

THINGS THAT GO

Many giant
machines move
very slowly.
This rocket
transporter is so
large it would
cover five tennis
courts.

Look at this
machine digging up coal. It moves
at the same speed as a tortoise.

Here is a combine harvester. It is moving slowly up the field.

This truck is so long it cannot get round the bend.

These machines move very fast.
When a powerboat moves along, the
front lifts out of the water. Look
for the waves made by the boat.

This car has a jet engine. In 1982
it reached a speed of over 600
miles an hour.

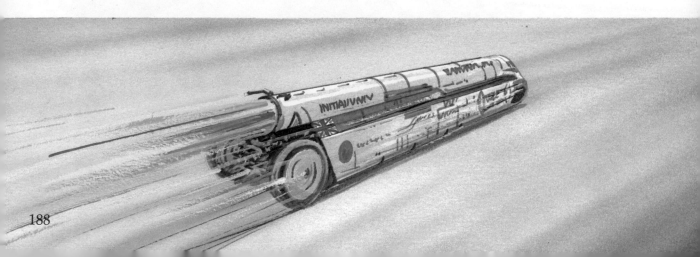

Some helicopters
go very quickly.
The fastest speed
is over 220 miles
an hour.

This was the first
plane to travel
faster than the
speed of sound.

Space rockets move
faster than all
these other things
that go. They have
to go fast to get
away from Earth
and into space.

Here are some things that go . . .
over ground.

This was the
first type of car
to have a roof
over the driver.

Here is the longest bus in the
world. It can carry 187 people.
It is as long as a tennis court.

Some things go . . . under ground.
Have you ever been in a tunnel?

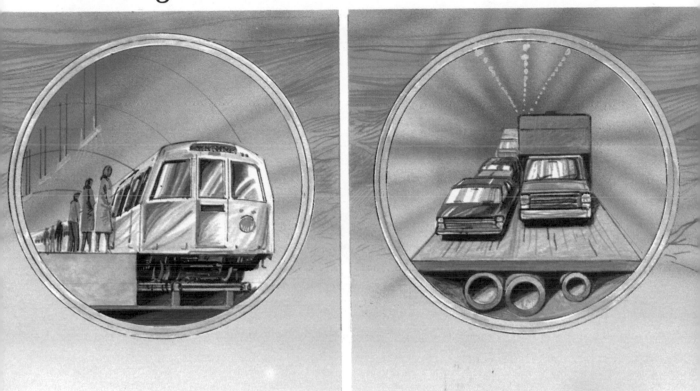

This buggy can go over snow and ice.

Look at this strange ship moving up and down on the waves. It is three sailing ships joined together.

This ship forces its way through frozen water.

The spacecraft splashed down into the sea. A helicopter is lifting it up.

There is a layer
of air between
the hovercraft and
the sea.

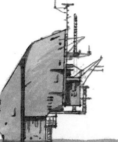

This ship is on end. It is
used for tests under the
water.

A submarine has tanks inside. When
the tanks fill with water, the
submarine sinks. It will rise again
if the water is pumped out.

All of these
things are in the
air. The balloon
has hot air inside
it. A glider has
wide wings but no
engine. It glides
through the air.
Can you see the
people with
parachutes? Would
you like to be
the pilot of the
very small plane?

This "Jumbo" jet is the heaviest plane ever built. It can carry 500 people.

This plane only flew once, in 1947. From the tip of one wing to the tip of the other is longer than any other plane.

Here are some things that go into space. Some spacecraft travel to other planets.

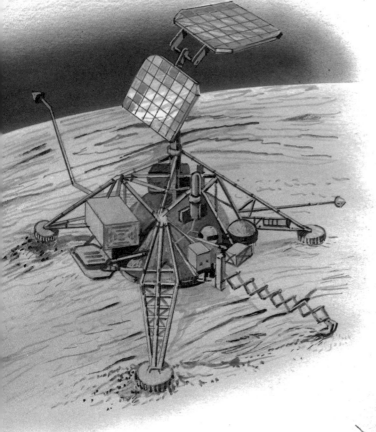

This robot spacecraft is on the Moon. It is digging up soil.

Look at this spacecraft. It is taking pictures of the planet Mercury.

Do you think this will happen in the future? The astronauts are working on the spacecraft. They are above another planet. Look for the other spacecraft.